h
Indian
cooking

Devagi Sanmugam

Bring the fabulous flavours of the Indian subcontinent into your
home with simple and easy homestyle recipes like Fragrant Eggplant
Curry, Tamarind Crab Soup and Fiery Chicken Vindaloo.
Indian Cooking has never been this easy—clear recipes,
step-by-step photographs and a complete glossary of ingredients
ensure fantastic results everytime.

PERIPLUS

Basic Indian Ingredients

Asafoetida is a pungent gum which is usually sold in powdered form. Use very small amounts—a pinch is enough. Keep well sealed when not in use.

Basmati rice is an Indian long-grain rice variety characterised by its thinness and fragrance. The grains stay whole and separate when cooked. Substitute long-grain Thai jasmine rice.

Cardamom pods are highly aromatic and contain tiny black seeds. If whole pods are used, they should be removed from the food before serving. If seeds are called for, lightly smash the pods and remove the seeds, discarding the pods. Ground cardamon is sold in packets or tins.

Chillies are indispensable in Asian cooking. The usual red and green finger-length chillies are moderately hot. Dried chillies are usually cut in lengths and soaked in warm water to soften before use. **Chilli powder,** a crucial ingredient in Indian cooking, is made from ground chillies.

Coconut milk is made by mixing freshly grated coconut flesh (available from Asian markets) with water and squeezing the liquid from the mixture. Add 125 ml ($^1/_2$ cup) water to 3 cups of grated fresh coconut. Squeeze and strain to obtain **thick coconut milk**. Add 625 ml ($2^1/_2$ cups) water to the grated coconut and squeeze again to obtain **thin coconut milk**. Cans or packets of concentrated coconut milk make a good substitute; dilute according to the instructions.

Cumin seeds (*jeera*) are pale brown and usually

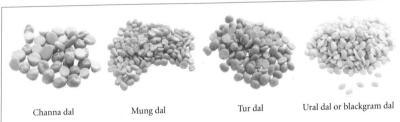

| Channa dal | Mung dal | Tur dal | Ural dal or blackgram dal |

Dal refers to a wide variety of split peas and pulses. **Channa dal** or Bengal gram resembles a yellow split pea but is smaller. Channa dal is also ground to make **Channa flour**. **Mung dal** is pale yellow and slightly elongated. **Tur dal** is a pale yellow lentil which is smaller than channa dal. **Urad dal** or **blackgram dal** is sold either with its black skin on or husked, when it is creamy white in colour.

partnered with coriander seeds in basic spice mixes. They impart an intense, earthy flavour to foods and are often dry-roasted or flash-cooked in oil to intensify their flavour.

Curry leaves are sold in sprigs containing 8–15 small, green leaves and are used to flavour Indian curries. There is no good substitute.

Curry powder is a readily available blend of Indian spices, and typically contains turmeric, coriander, chillies, cumin, mustard, ginger, fenugreek, garlic, cloves, salt, and any number of other spices.

Garam masala is an Indian blend of powdered spices, usually including cinnamon, cardamon, cloves, fennel and black pepper. Pre-blended garam masala can be bought from any

store specializing in spices. Store in an airtight jar away from heat or sunlight.

Fennel seeds look like cumin seeds but are larger and paler. They add a sweet fragrance to Indian dishes, with a flavour similar to liquorice or anise. The seeds are used whole or ground.

Fenugreek is a small almost square, yellowish-brown seed. It is strongly flavoured and easily available from Indian food-stores and supermarkets. The taste is somewhat like burnt maple, sweet yet bitter, with a hint of celery. In addition to curries, fenugreek will enhance meats, poultry and vegetables. Too much of it will cause foods to become bitter, so use with caution.

Ghee is a rich clarified butter oil with the milk

solids removed that is the main oil used in Indian cooking. Substitute with vegetable oil or butter.

Mustard seeds are small brownish-black seeds that are commonly used in Indian cooking, imparting a nutty flavour to dishes.

Tamarind is commonly available in the form of semi-dried pulp. It must be soaked in water, mashed, squeezed and strained to yield a sour juice that is added to soups and sauces. All solids and pulp should be strained and discarded from the liquid before use.

Turmeric resembles ginger when fresh but is commonly sold in dried form as a yellow powder. Turmeric turns dishes yellow and has a mild flavour.

Sweet Tomato Date Chutney

2 tablespoons oil
$^1/_2$ teaspoon urad dal
$^1/_2$ teaspoon mustard seeds
$^1/_2$ teaspoon cumin seeds
$^1/_2$ teaspoon fennel seeds
1 bay leaf
75 g ($^1/_4$ cup) tamarind pulp mixed with 50 ml
  ($^1/_4$ cup) water, mashed and strained
500 g ($2^3/_4$ cups) diced fresh tomatoes,
  or canned whole tomatoes
200 g (1 cup) sugar
1 red finger-length chilli, finely sliced
125 g (1 cup) pitted dates, quartered
$^3/_4$ teaspoon salt

Serves 6
Preparation time: **10 mins**
Cooking time: **45 mins**

1 Heat the oil in a wok or skillet over low heat and stir-fry the dal and spices and the bay leaf until aromatic, 4 to 5 minutes.
2 Add the remaining ingredients, bring to a boil, then lower the heat and simmer until the chutney thickens, about 45 minutes. Allow to cool, then store in a sealed container in the refrigerator.

Sweet Lime Chutney

500 g (1 lb) limes, deseeded and finely chopped
2 tablespoons salt
2 onions, chopped (about $1^1/_2$ cups)
2 tablespoons mustard seeds, roasted and coarsely ground
300 g ($1^1/_2$ cups) sugar
300 ml ($1^1/_4$ cups) white vinegar
2 teaspoons chilli powder
1 teaspoon turmeric powder
100 g (scant $^3/_4$ cup) raisins

Serves 6
Preparation time: **15 mins**
Cooking time: **1 hour**
       15 mins

1 Place the chopped lime pieces in a stainless steel saucepan. Sprinkle with the salt and mix well. Add all the remaining ingredients and simmer over low heat until the lime pieces become tender and the chutney thickens, about 1 hour 15 minutes. Serve as an accompaniment.

Spicy Mango Coconut Chutney

200 g (1$^1/_4$ cups) peeled and diced unripe mango
250 g (2$^1/_2$ cups) grated fresh coconut
4 green finger-length chillies, cut into lengths
$^1/_2$ teaspoon salt
1$^1/_2$ tablespoons oil
$^1/_2$ teaspoon urad dal
$^1/_2$ teaspoon mustard seeds
1 sprig curry leaves
$^1/_4$ teaspoon asafoetida

Serves 6
Preparation time: **10 mins**
Cooking time: **10 mins**

1 Coarsely grind the diced mango, coconut, green chillies and salt in a blender and set aside.
2 In a small saucepan, heat the oil and fry the urad dal over low heat until golden brown. Add the mustard seeds and curry leaves and fry until the seeds pop. Add the asafoetida, mix well and turn off the heat.
3 Add the fried spices to the ground ingredients and mix well. Serve as an accompaniment to rice or breads.

Coriander Coconut Chutney

100 g (2 cups) fresh coriander leaves, chopped
500 g (5 cups) grated fresh coconut
4 green fnger-length chillies, sliced
  into lengths
4 tablespoons lime juice
3 slices ginger
1 teaspoon salt
125 ml ($^1/_2$ cup) water

Place all the ingredients in a food processor or blender and process until smooth. Serve with thosai, idli or any savoury snacks.

Serves 6
Preparation time: **20 mins**
Cooking time: **nil**

Plain Basmati Rice

750 ml (3 cups) water
Pinch of salt
1 teaspoon ghee or oil
400 g (2 cups) uncooked
    basmati rice, washed,
    soaked for 20 minutes
    and drained

Place the water, salt and ghee or oil in a pot and bring to a boil over high heat. Add the drained rice, reduce the heat and cook, covered, for 10 minutes, or until done. Turn off the heat and let the rice stand, covered, for 10 minutes before gently stirring it with a fork to separate the grains. Alternatively, place all the ingredients in a rice cooker and cook according to the manufacturer's instructions.

Serves 4
Preparation time: **25 mins**
Cooking time: **20 mins**

Fragrant Mint Rice

150 g (3$^1/_2$ cups) mint
    leaves
2 green finger-length
    chillies
3 cloves garlic
2 cm ($^3/_4$ in) ginger
750 ml (3 cups) water
1 tablespoon ghee or oil
1 teaspoon cumin seeds
400 g (2 cups) uncooked
    basmati rice, washed,
    soaked for 20 minutes
    and drained
1$^1/_2$ teaspoons salt

1 Place the mint leaves, green chillies, garlic, ginger and 250 ml (1 cup) of the water in a blender and blend until fine. Set aside.
2 Heat the ghee or oil in a wok and fry the cumin seeds until aromatic. Add the drained rice and stir-fry for 2 minutes. Remove from the heat and set aside.
3 Combine the blended ingredients with the remaining water in a large pan and bring to a boil. Add the stir-fried rice and salt, cover and cook for 10 minutes or until the rice is done. Set aside, still covered, for 10 minutes then fluff the rice up with a fork or the back of a wooden spoon. Alternatively, place the blended ingredients with the remainder of the water in a rice cooker and cook according to the manufacturer's instructions.

Serves 4
Preparation time: **30 mins**
Cooking time: **15 mins**

Potato Puri

2 medium potatoes (300 g/10 oz)
200 g (1 1/3 cups) flour
5 tablespoons plain yoghurt
1 teaspoon salt
6 tablespoons water
Oil for deep-frying

1 Place the potatoes in a pan, cover with water, and
bring to a boil, then simmer until cooked, about 10 to
15 minutes. When the potatoes are done, peel and
mash until free of lumps. Set aside.
2 Sift the flour into a bowl and add the yoghurt, salt
and mashed potatoes.
3 Mix by hand to form a soft dough, adding sufficient
water to soften. Knead for 10 minutes then set aside
for 10 minutes.
4 Divide the mixture into 12 equal portions. Place a
portion on a rolling board dusted with flour then roll
it out into a pancake about 10 cm (4 in) in diameter.
5 Heat the oil in a wok until very hot and then deep-
fry 1 or 2 puris at a time until golden brown.
6 Remove from the oil and drain on paper towels.
Serve with Vegetarian Dal Curry (page 23) or with
a chutney (see pages 4 and 5).

Makes 12 pieces
Preparation time: **25 mins**
Cooking time: **20 mins**

Chapati (Whole Wheat Flat Bread)

250 g (2 cups) fine
  wholemeal (*atta*) flour
$^1/_2$ teaspoon salt
1 teaspoon ghee or butter
150 ml ($^2/_3$ cup) water
Extra flour for dusting

Atta flour is a form of
whole wheat flour. It is
made from durum wheat
that is ground very fine,
with some of the bran
included. Breads made
from atta flour include
chapati and roti.

1 Sift the flour, salt and ghee into a mixing bowl.
Make a well in the centre and add the water.
2 Mix by hand to form a soft dough, then knead it for
10 minutes on a lightly-floured work surface. Set aside
for 15 minutes.
3 Divide the dough into 6 portions. Flatten each piece
on the palm of your hand, pressing it with the fingers.
Place it on a rolling board dusted with flour and roll
into a thin pancake, about 13 cm (5 in) in diameter.
4 Heat a skillet or a griddle. Place the rolled chapati on it.
5 Cook on medium heat for 2 minutes. When one side
dries and tiny bubbles begin to appear, flip it over and
cook until brown spots form on the underside.
Remove and serve immediately.

Makes 6 pieces
Preparation time: **20 mins**   Cooking time: **15 mins**

Make a well in the centre of of the flour and pour in the water.

Flatten each piece of dough on the palm of your hand then press flat with fingers.

Roll each portion of dough into a thin pancake, about 13 cm (5 in) in diameter.

Cook for 2 minutes until one side dries and bubbles begin to appear, then flip.

Garlic Curry

3 tablespoons oil
2 tablespoons coriander seeds
8 dried red chillies
2 tablespoons channa dal
$1/2$ teaspoon asafoetida
$1/2$ teaspoon black peppercorns
160 g ($1^2/3$ cups) fresh grated coconut
1 teaspoon mustard seeds
$1/2$ teaspoon fenugreek
2 sprigs curry leaves
250 g (9 oz) whole garlic cloves, peeled
$1/2$ teaspoon turmeric powder
75 g ($1/4$ cup) tamarind pulp mixed with 500 ml (2 cups) water, mashed and strained
1 teaspoon salt

1 Heat 1 tablespoon of the oil in a wok or skillet and stir-fry the coriander seeds, dried chillies, channa dal, asafoetida and black peppercorns until aromatic. Add the coconut and fry for another 2 minutes or until the coconut is light brown. Remove from the heat, cool thoroughly and then grind to a paste in a blender or food processor.
2 In a medium saucepan, heat the remaining 2 tablespoons of oil and fry the mustard seeds, fenugreek and curry leaves. When aromatic, add the whole garlic cloves and fry well for 5 minutes until lightly browned.
3 Add the rest of the ingredients, bring to a boil and simmer until the curry thickens, about 12 minutes. Serve with rice.

Serves 4
Preparation time: **20 mins**
Cooking time: **30 mins**

Stir-fried Ladies Fingers

2 tablespoons oil
$1/2$ teaspoon mustard seeds
$1/2$ teaspoon cumin seeds
1 onion, sliced
2 sprigs curry leaves
300 g (10 oz) ladies fingers (okra)
$1/2$ teaspoon turmeric powder
$1/2$ teaspoon cumin powder
1 teaspoon chilli powder
$1/4$ teaspoon water
1 teaspoon salt

1 Cut the ladies fingers into sections.
2 Heat the oil in a wok and stir-fry the mustard seeds and cumin seeds until aromatic. Add the onion and curry leaves and fry until the onion turns golden brown.
3 Add the rest of the ingredients and stir-fry until the ladies fingers are cooked. Serve as a side dish to Salt Fish Mango Curry (page 43).

Serves 4
Preparation time: **10 mins**
Cooking time: **10 mins**

Spicy Tomato Soup

500 g (1 lb) ripe toma-
toes, blanched, skins
removed or 1 can
whole tomatoes
1$^1/_4$ litres (5 cups) water
$^1/_2$ teaspoon turmeric
powder
1 teaspoon ground
cumin
$^1/_2$ teaspoon chilli
powder
3 cloves garlic, ground
to a paste
2 cm (1 in) ginger,
ground to a paste
1$^1/_2$ teaspoons salt
2 tablespoons oil
2 small cinnamon sticks
5 cardamom pods
5 cloves
1 teaspoon fennel
1 onion, thinly sliced
2 sprigs curry leaves
40 g ($^3/_4$ cup) chopped
coriander leaves
1 spring onion, chopped

1 In a large pot, place the tomatoes, water, turmeric, cumin, chilli, garlic, ginger and salt. Bring to a boil and simmer for 15 minutes.

2 Meanwhile, heat the oil in a wok or skillet. Stir-fry the cinnamon, cardamoms, cloves and fennel until aromatic. Add the sliced onion and curry leaves, and stir-fry for another 2 minutes until the onion is translucent. Transfer to the soup.

3 Boil the soup for a further 5 minutes. Remove from the heat and garnish with the coriander leaves and spring onion.

This soup is equally delicious served with rice or bread. To prepare **Spicy Fish Head Soup**, add approximately 500 g (1 lb) fish head, chopped into large pieces, to the soup together with the fried spices in Step 2. Boil for 10 minutes or until the fish is cooked.

Serves 4
Preparation time: **25 mins**
Cooking time: **20 mins**

Sambar (Vegetable Stew)

200 g (1 cup) tur dal, washed and drained
1 small onion, sliced
1 small can (180 g/6 oz) stewed tomatoes
2 sprigs curry leaves
$1/2$ teaspoon turmeric powder
1 litre (4 cups) water
1 teaspoon salt
750 g (8 cups) mixed diced vegetables (such as carrot,
  potatoes, eggplant, cauliflower and pumpkin)
$1/2$ teaspoon chilli powder
100 g (1 cup) grated fresh coconut, ground to a smooth
  paste in a blender with 100 ml ($1/3$ cup) water
$1/2$ teaspoon sugar
25 g ($1/2$ cup) coriander leaves, chopped
75 g ($1/4$ cup) tamarind pulp mixed with 250 ml (1 cup)
  water, mashed and strained to obtain juice
$1 1/2$ teaspoons sambar powder (see page 18)
2 tablespoons oil or ghee
1 teaspoon mustard seeds
2 dried red chillies
$1/4$ teaspoon asafoetida

1 Place the tur dal, onions, tomatoes, curry leaves,
turmeric, water and salt into a pan and boil for about
15 minutes, or until partially cooked.
2 Add to the mixture any hard root vegetables which
may need a longer cooking time. Stir in the chilli
powder, ground coconut, sugar, tamarind juice and
sambar powder and cook for 20 minutes until the
vegetables are slightly softened and the dal broken up.
3 Add the rest of the vegetables and simmer a further
10 minutes.
4 Meanwhile, in a separate pan, heat the oil and stir-
fry the mustard seeds, dried chillies and asafoetida
until aromatic. Transfer to the simmering stew. Cook
for a further 2 minutes, season to taste and serve.

Serves 6
Preparation time: **20 min**   Cooking time: **50 mins**

Fragrant Eggplant Curry

4 teaspoons sambar
  powder (see note)
1 teaspoon salt
500 g (1 lb) long purple
  eggplants
5 tablespoons oil
1 teaspoon mustard
  seeds
1 teaspoon cumin seeds
1 onion, sliced
2 sprigs curry leaves
2 tomatoes, chopped
75 g ($^1/_4$ cup) tamarind
  pulp mixed with 500 ml
  (2 cups) water, mashed
  and strained to obtain
  juice
$^1/_2$ teaspoon salt
175 g ($1^3/_4$ cups) grated
  fresh coconut ground to
  a smooth paste with
  125 ml ($^1/_2$ cup) water

Serves 5
Preparation time: 20 mins
Cooking time: 25 mins

1 Make 3–4 deep slits in the sides of each eggplant.
Mix 2 teaspoons of the sambar powder with the
salt and coat the eggplants inside and out. In a large
skillet or wok, heat 3 tablespoons of the oil and
toss the eggplants quickly to brown and soften them
slightly. Set aside.
2 Heat the remaining 2 tablespoons of oil in a large
saucepan, add the mustard and cumin seeds and stir-fry
until aromatic. Add the sliced onion and curry leaves
and stir-fry until golden brown, about 5 minutes.
3 Add the tomatoes and the remaining sambar
powder and stir-fry for 1 minute. Reduce the heat and
stir-fry until the oil separates, about 5 minutes.
4 Add the tamarind juice and salt and bring to a boil,
then simmer about 3 minutes.
5 Add the fried eggplants and cook until the eggplants
are soft. Add the ground coconut and simmer for
about a further 2 minutes, then serve hot with rice.

Sambar powder is also known as *sambar podi*—a
tart powder mixture containing roasted ground dal,
coriander, cumin, black pepper and fenugreek. It is
readily available from Indian grocers and is popular in
southern Indian vegetarian cooking.

Spicy Rasam Carrot Soup

100 g ($^1/_2$ cup) tur dal
1$^1/_2$ litres (6 cups) water
$^1/_2$ teaspoon turmeric
  powder
200 g (2 cups) grated
  carrot
150 g ($^3/_4$ cup) chopped
  tomato or canned
  whole tomatoes
1$^1/_2$ teaspoons salt
2 tablespoons oil
1 teaspoon mustard seeds
$^1/_2$ teaspoon cumin seeds
2 dried red chillies, cut
  into pieces
2 sprigs curry leaves
$^1/_4$ teaspoon asafoetida
  powder
125 ml ($^1/_2$ cup) fresh
  lime juice
250 ml (1 cup) water
25 g ($^1/_2$ cup) coriander
  leaves, chopped

Rasam Powder
3 dried red chillies, cut
  into pieces
$^1/_2$ teaspoon cumin seeds
$^1/_2$ tablespoon
  coriander seeds
$^1/_2$ tablespoon tur dal
2 teaspoons black
  peppercorns
$^1/_2$ teaspoon channa dal

1 Place the tur dal, water and turmeric in a pan, bring to a boil and simmer until the dal is very soft, about 25 minutes. Drain, reserving both the liquid and the dal. Mash the dal, then return it to the soup.

2 Meanwhile, prepare the Rasam Powder by grinding all the ingredients to a fine powder in a blender or spice grinder.

3 Add the Rasam Powder, carrot, tomato and salt to the soup. Return to the boil, and simmer for about 2 minutes.

4 Meanwhile, in another small pan, heat the oil and stir-fry the mustard, cumin and dried chillies until the chillies turn brown. Stir in the curry leaves and asafoetida powder, then transfer the fried spices to the soup.

5 Add the lime juice, water and coriander leaves. Just as the soup returns to the boil, switch off the heat and serve immediately.

Serves 4
Preparation time: 10 mins
Cooking time: 30 mins

Vegetarian Dal Curry

300 g (1 1/2 cups)
   tur dal, soaked for
   3 hours
3 tablespoons channa
   dal, soaked for
   3 hours
2 green finger-length
   chillies, cut into lengths
1/2 teaspoon turmeric
   powder
1/2 teaspoon asafoetida
1/2 teaspoon salt
100 g (1 cup) finely
   grated carrot
10 dried red chillies,
   soaked
3/4 teaspoon fenugreek
75 g (1/4 cup) tamarind
   pulp mixed with 1 litre
   (4 cups) water, mashed
   and strained to obtain
   juice
2 tablespoons oil
1 teaspoon cumin seeds
1/2 teaspoon mustard
   seeds
2 sprigs curry leaves

1 Drain both the tur and channa dals and grind them to a paste in a blender or food processor with the green chillies, turmeric powder, asafoetida and salt (it may be easier to do this in several batches). Stir in the grated carrot and mix well.

2 Shape the ground mixture into small balls and place on a lightly oiled tray. Steam for 10 minutes. Remove from the steamer and set aside.

3 Grind the dried chillies and fenugreek with the tamarind juice in a blender and set aside.

4 In a saucepan, heat the oil and stir-fry the cumin, mustard and the curry leaves until aromatic.

5 Add in the tamarind juice mixture, bring to a boil, then reduce the heat and simmer for about 10 minutes.

6 Add the steamed dal balls. Return to the boil and simmer for a further 5 minutes.

Serves 4
Preparation time: 30 mins plus 3 hours soaking
Cooking time: 25 mins

Banana Stem Curry

125 g (⁵/₈ cup) mung dal
1 litre (4 cups) water
1 teaspoon turmeric powder
4 cloves garlic
750 g (1¹/₂ lbs) chopped banana stem, bottle gourd or bitter gourd
1 tablespoon vegetable curry powder
75 g (¹/₄ cup) tamarind pulp mixed with 200 ml (³/₄ cup) water, mashed and strained to obtain juice
1 teaspoon salt

Spice Mix
2 tablespoons ghee or butter
¹/₂ teaspoon mustard seeds
¹/₂ teaspoon urad dal
¹/₂ teaspoon fennel seeds
¹/₂ teaspoon cumin seeds
1 onion, sliced
2 sprigs curry leaves

1 Dry-roast the mung dal over low heat in a wok or skillet until fragrant. Wash well and drain. Place the mung dal, water, turmeric and garlic in a medium saucepan, bring to a boil and simmer until the dal is soft, about 15 minutes.

2 Add the banana stem or gourd pieces, vegetable curry powder and tamarind juice. Return to the boil and simmer for 5 minutes, or until the vegetable is cooked.

3 Prepare the Spice Mix by heating the ghee in a separate pan. Fry the mustard seeds, urad dal, fennel and cumin seeds until fragrant. Add the onion slices and curry leaves and stir-fry until golden brown.

4 Transfer the Spice Mix to the boiling vegetables and let the curry simmer for another 2 minutes. Season to taste with salt.

Banana stem is the centre of the young banana palm. To prepare, peel off the outer layers of the banana stem to reach the tender moist inner part, cut in half lengthwise before chopping finely.

The **bottle gourd** is a common vegetable in Indian cooking. It is yellowish green, having the shape of a bottle. It has a white pulp, with white seeds embedded in a spongy flesh.

Serves 4
Preparation time: **15 mins**   Cooking time: **30 mins**

Discard the outer layers of the banana stem then chop the tender inner part finely.

Dry-roast the mung dal in a wok then wash well and drain before using.

Vegetables in Spicy Coconut Milk

2 tablespoons oil
1 teaspoon fenugreek
  seeds
$^1/_2$ teaspoon cumin seeds
2 slices ginger
2 red finger-length chillies,
  halved lengthwise
750 ml (3 cups) thin
  coconut milk
$^1/_2$ teaspoon turmeric
  powder
$^1/_2$ teaspoon cumin
  powder
1$^1/_2$ teaspoons salt
150 g (5 oz) small
  prawns (optional)
125 ml ($^1/_2$ cup) thick
  coconut milk
500 g (1 lb) mustard
  leaves or spinach,
  washed and sliced

1 Heat the oil in a wok over medium heat and fry the fenugreek and cumin seeds until aromatic. Add the ginger and red chillies, stir-fry briefly then add the thin coconut milk, turmeric and cumin powders, and salt.

2 Bring to a boil and simmer for about 3 minutes, then add the prawns (if using), and cook for a further 2 minutes.

3 Add the thick coconut milk and vegetables. Return to the boil, then remove from the heat and serve with rice.

Serves 4
Preparation time: **10 mins**
Cooking time: **10 mins**

Potato and Baby Whitebait Masala

3 tablespoons oil
1 teaspoon urad dal
1 teaspoon fennel seeds
1 onion, peeled and sliced
2 sprigs curry leaves
3 large or 4 medium pota-
  toes, peeled and cubed
50 g ($^1/_2$ cup) small
  whitebait (*ikan bilis*),
  rinsed and drained
1 teaspoon turmeric
  powder
1 teaspoon cumin powder
1$^1/_2$ tablespoons chilli
  powder
300 ml (1$^1/_4$ cups) water
2 eggs, lightly beaten with
  $^1/_2$ teaspoon salt

1 Heat the oil in a wok over medium heat and stir-fry the urad dal and fennel until aromatic.

2 Add the onion and curry leaves and stir-fry until the onions brown lightly, about 2 minutes.

3 Add the remaining ingredients except the eggs. Cover and cook until the potatoes are done and the gravy is dry, about 10 to 15 minutes.

4 Move the potatoes to the side of the pan and pour in the egg. Let the egg set lightly then stir in the rest of the ingredients. Stir-fry until the egg is set and well mixed with all the ingredients.

Serves 4
Preparation time: **15 mins**
Cooking time: **15 mins**

Spinach with Dal and Dried Prawn Curry

200 g (1 cup) tur dal, washed and drained
1 teaspoon turmeric powder
5 cloves garlic, peeled
2 green finger-length chillies
1 teaspoon ghee or butter
1 litre (4 cups) water
2 tablespoons oil
1 teaspoon mustard seeds
1 teaspoon fennel seeds
2 dried red chillies, cut into pieces
3 tablespoons dried prawns, soaked for 5 minutes,
   drained and pounded
1 onion, peeled and sliced
500 g (1 lb) washed and finely chopped spinach
100 g ($^1/_3$ cup) tamarind pulp mixed with 250 ml
   (1 cup) water, stirred and strained to obtain juice
1 teaspoon salt

1 In a large saucepan, cook the tur dal, turmeric powder, garlic, chillies, ghee and water over high heat until the dal is soft, about 30 minutes.
2 Meanwhile, in a separate pan, heat the oil and stir-fry the mustard and fennel seeds until aromatic. Add the dried chillies, dried prawns and onion to the spices and stir-fry until aromatic and the dried chillies turn brown. Remove from the heat and set aside.
3 When the dal is ready, add the spinach, tamarind juice and salt to the saucepan. Simmer until the spinach is almost cooked, about 2 minutes.
4 Add the fried spices to the dal and spinach and simmer for a further 2 minutes.

Serves 4
Preparation time: **15 mins**
Cooking time: **40 mins**

Prawn Curry

750 g (1¹/₂ lbs) large prawns, shelled, cleaned and deveined
1 tablespoon chilli powder
2 tablespoons fish curry powder
¹/₂ teaspoon turmeric powder
3 cm (1 in) fresh ginger, peeled and cut into strips
2 cloves garlic, pounded
3 tablespoons oil
¹/₂ teaspoon mustard seeds
1 teaspoon cumin seeds
1 onion, thinly sliced
2 sprigs curry leaves
250 ml (1 cup) thick coconut milk
2 small cucumbers, deseeded and cubed
2 green finger-length chillies, cut into lengths
1 tablespoon white vinegar or lime juice
Salt to taste

1 In a bowl, combine the prawns, chilli, curry and turmeric powders, ginger and garlic. Set aside for 5 minutes to marinate.
2 Heat the oil in a wok or skillet and stir-fry the mustard and cumin seeds over medium heat until aromatic, about 5 minutes. Add the onion and curry leaves and stir-fry until the onion is golden brown, about 4 minutes. Add the prawns and stir-fry a further 4 minutes.
3 Add the coconut milk, cucumber, chillies and vinegar. Bring to a boil, and simmer gently, stirring continuously for 3 minutes. Add salt to taste and serve hot with rice.

Serves 4
Preparation time: **10 mins**
Cooking time: **10 mins**

Curried Crabs

3 tablespoons oil
1 teaspoon urad dal
1 teaspoon fennel seeds
1 teaspoon cumin seeds
1 onion, peeled and sliced
1 sprig curry leaves
2 tablespoons seafood curry powder
1 teaspoon turmeric powder
2 teaspoons ground almonds
1 teaspoon salt
1 red finger-length chilli, cut lengthwise
125 g ($^1/_2$ cup) sliced tomatoes or canned peeled tomatoes
1 teaspoon tomato purée or ketchup
375 ml (1$^1/_2$ cups) thin coconut milk, fresh milk or diluted evaporated milk
125 ml ($^1/_2$ cup) water
750 g (1$^1/_2$ lb) crabs, cleaned and halved or quartered, claws and legs cracked

1 In a large deep pan or wok, heat the oil and stir-fry the urad dal over medium heat until golden brown, about 4 minutes. Add the fennel and cumin and fry until aromatic.
2 Add the onion slices and curry leaves and stir-fry until the onion is golden brown, about 2 minutes.
3 Add the remaining ingredients except for the crab. Stir well to combine then add the crabs. Cook on medium high heat for another 20 minutes or until the crabs are done, stirring constantly to keep the spices from burning at the bottom of the pan.

Serves 4
Preparation time: **20 mins**
Cooking time: **30 mins**

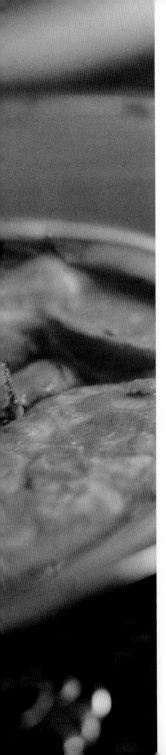

Kerala Fish Curry

2 tablespoons oil
$^1/_2$ teaspoon mustard seeds
$^1/_2$ teaspoon fenugreek
100 g (1 cup) peeled and sliced shallots
3 cm (1 in) fresh ginger, sliced
2 green finger-length chillies, cut in half lengthwise
2 sprigs curry leaves
2 tablespoons coriander powder
1 teaspoon turmeric powder
1 teaspoon cumin powder
$1^1/_2$ tablespoons chilli powder
100 g ($^1/_3$ cup) tamarind pulp mixed with 375 ml
   ($1^1/_2$ cups) water, stirred and strained
200 g (7 oz) ladies' fingers (okra), cut into lengths
2 ripe tomatoes, quartered
500 g (1 lb) fish steaks, sliced $1^1/_2$ cm ($^1/_2$ in) thick
250 ml (1 cup) thick coconut milk
1 teaspoon salt, or to taste

1 In a large saucepan, heat the oil over medium heat and stir-fry the mustard seeds and fenugreek until aromatic, about 4 minutes. Add the shallots, ginger, green chillies and curry leaves. Stir-fry until the shallots turn light brown, about 3 to 4 minutes.
2 Add the coriander, turmeric, cumin and chilli powders and the tamarind juice. Cook for a further 5 minutes, stirring well.
3 Add the ladies' fingers and tomatoes, simmer for 3 minutes, then add the fish steaks. Simmer until the fish is cooked, about 5 minutes.
4 Stir in the coconut milk, return to the boil and simmer for approximately 1 minute. Season with salt to taste, then serve.

Serves 4
Preparation time: **20 mins**
Cooking time: **20 mins**

Swordfish Curry

4 tablespoons oil
8 cloves
8 cardamom pods
2 short cinnamon sticks
2 onions, peeled and
  sliced
2 sprigs curry leaves
2 cloves garlic
2 cm ($3/4$ in) ginger,
  pounded to a paste
$1/2$ teaspoon turmeric
  powder
$1^1/_2$ tablespoons chilli
  powder
$1^1/_2$ tablespoons coriander powder
1 teaspoon cumin
  powder
4 tablespoons grated
  fresh coconut ground
  into a fine paste with
  100 ml ($1/_3$ cup) water
500 ml (2 cups) thick
  coconut milk or water
125 g ($1/_2$ cup) diced
  tomatoes or canned
  tomatoes
$1/_2$ tablespoon salt
25 g ($1/_2$ cup) chopped
  coriander leaves
500 g (1 lb) swordfish or
  shark cutlets, cut into
  chunks (substitute with
  any oily fish)

1 Heat the oil in a wok over medium heat and stir-fry
the cloves, cardamoms and cinnamon sticks until aromatic, about 3 to 4 minutes. Add the onions and
curry leaves and stir-fry until golden brown, about
2 minutes.
2 Stir in the garlic-ginger paste, chilli powder, coriander,
cumin and ground coconut. Stir-fry over low heat
until the oil separates, about 3 minutes.
3 Stir in the coconut milk (or water), tomatoes, salt
and chopped coriander and bring to a boil. Add
the fish pieces to the curry, return to the boil and
simmer until the fish is done, about 8 to 10 minutes.

Serves 4
Preparation time: **15 mins**
Cooking time: **15 mins**

Tamarind Crab Soup

500 g (1 lb) crabs, cleaned, quartered and slightly
  smashed
2 ripe tomatoes, blended (to yield $^1/_2$ cup)
1 teaspoon tomato purée
5 cloves garlic, pounded
150 g ($^1/_2$ cup) tamarind pulp mixed with 500 ml
  (2 cups) water, mashed and strained to obtain juice
1 litre (4 cups) water
1 teaspoon turmeric powder
$1^1/_2$ teaspoons black peppercorns, crushed
1 teaspoon cumin powder
25 g ($^1/_2$ cup) chopped coriander leaves
$1^1/_2$ teaspoons salt

Spice Mix
2 tablespoons oil
1 teaspoon cumin seeds
$^1/_2$ teaspoon fenugreek
$^1/_2$ teaspoon mustard seeds
2 sprigs curry leaves
2 dried red chillies, cut into lengths

1 Place all the ingredients, except the Spice Mix, into
a medium saucepan, bring to a boil over high heat
and simmer for 15 minutes.
2 Meanwhile, prepare the Spice Mix in a separate pan
by adding all the ingredients and stir-frying gently
until aromatic.
3 Transfer the spices to the soup and cook for a
further 2 minutes before removing from the heat.

Serves 4–6
Preparation time: **25 mins**
Cooking time: **20 mins**

Tanjore Fried Fish

2 onions
500 g (1 lb) fish slices
4 cloves garlic, pounded
1 sprig curry leaves, finely shredded
1 teaspoon fennel, coarsely pounded
1 tablespoon semolina
$1^1/_2$ tablespoons chilli powder
1 teaspoon turmeric powder
1 teaspoon cumin powder
1 teaspoon fennel powder
$1^1/_2$ teaspoons salt
2 tablespoons tamarind juice or lime juice
3 tablespoons water
Oil for frying

1 Blend the onions in a food processor until fine. Place the onion together with the fish and all the other ingredients, except the oil, in a bowl and mix well. Set aside for 30 minutes to marinate.
2 Cover the base of a skillet or wok with oil, transfer the fish slices to the pan and shallow fry over medium heat on both sides until the fish is cooked and crisp on the outside, about 8 to 10 minutes.
3 Drain on absorbent paper and serve.

Serves 5
Preparation time: **40 mins**
Cooking time: **13 mins**

Masala Grilled Fish

4 cloves garlic
4 shallots, peeled
1 cm (¹/₂ in) ginger
1 tablespoon fresh coriander leaves, finely chopped
1 teaspoon garam masala
1¹/₂ teaspoon chilli powder
¹/₄ teaspoon turmeric powder
1 teaspoon salt
2 tablespoons freshly squeezed lemon juice
500 g (1 lb) whole fish, cleaned, deep cuts made in flesh on both sides
1 tablespoon ghee (or oil)

1 Grind the garlic, shallots, ginger and coriander leaves to a paste in a mortar or blender. Mix the paste together in a wide bowl together with all the other ingredients except the fish and ghee.

2 Line an oven-proof dish with banana leaf or tin foil. Spread some of the spice mixture on the banana leaf or tin foil. Place the fish on it and spoon the remaining spice mixture over the fish, rubbing it into the cuts and stuffing some of the mixture into the cavities.

3 Grill the fish for about 7 to 8 minutes on each side, basting it occasionally with ghee or oil.

Serves: 4
Preparation time: **15 mins**
Cover time: **15 mins**

Salt Fish Mango Curry

300 g (10 oz) dried salted fish
250 g (1¹/₂ cups) peeled and cubed unripe green
    mango, from 4 small mangoes
1¹/₂ teaspoons chilli powder
2 tablespoons coriander powder
1 teaspoon turmeric powder
1 teaspoon cumin powder
2 onions, peeled and sliced
2 teaspoons minced ginger
1 tablespoon minced garlic
6 green finger-length chillies, halved lengthwise
2 sprigs curry leaves
500 ml (2 cups) water
250 g (2¹/₂ cups) grated fresh coconut, coarsely ground
2 tablespoons oil
1 teaspoon mustard seeds
¹/₄ teaspoon fenugreek
2 dried red chillies, cut into pieces
1 onion, peeled and sliced

1 Soak the salted fish in water for 10 minutes to remove
some of the salt. Drain, then cut into small cubes.
2 Place the fish, mango, chilli, coriander, turmeric and
cumin powders, onions, ginger, garlic, green chillies,
curry leaves and water into a large saucepan. Cover
and cook over medium heat until the fish is soft and
flakes easily with a fork, about 15 to 20 minutes.
3 Stir in the grated coconut and cook until the gravy
thickens, about 5 to 10 minutes.
4 Meanwhile, in a separate pan, heat the oil and stir-
fry the mustard seeds, fenugreek and dried chillies
until aromatic. Add the onion and stir-fry until it
browns lightly.
5 Transfer the mixture to the simmering fish curry,
stir to mix well and remove from the heat. Serve with
Sweet Tomato Date Chutney (see page 4) and rice.

Serves 4
Preparation time: **25 mins**
Cooking time: **40 mins**

Fish Sothi Curry

2 tablespoons oil
1 teaspoon fenugreek
$1/2$ teaspoon mustard seeds
$1/2$ teaspoon cumin seeds
1 onion, peeled and sliced
2 red finger-length chillies, cut lengthwise
1 sprig curry leaves
$1/2$ teaspoon turmeric powder
1 teaspoon cumin powder
$1/2$ teaspoon ground white pepper
1 teaspoon salt
1 ripe tomato, quartered
750 ml (3 cups) thin coconut milk
500 g (1 lb) fish steaks, sliced thickly
250 ml (1 cup) thick coconut milk

1 Heat the oil in a wok over medium heat and stir-fry the fenugreek, mustard and cumin seeds until aromatic, about 4 minutes.
2 Add the onion, red chillies and curry leaves and stir-fry until lightly browned, about 2 minutes.
3 Stir in the turmeric and cumin, pepper, salt, tomato and thin coconut milk. Bring to a boil and simmer for about 5 minutes.
4 Add the fish steaks and thick coconut milk and return to the boil. Simmer, stirring occasionally, until the fish is cooked, about 7 to 8 minutes, then serve.

Serves 4
Preparation time: **15 mins**
Cooking time: **20 mins**

Prawn Fritters

60 g ($^1/_2$ cup) rice flour
75 g ($^1/_2$ cup) plain flour
90 g ($^1/_2$ cup) semolina
 flour
50 g ($^1/_2$ cup) channa
 flour
1 teaspoon baking powder
1$^1/_2$ teaspoons salt
1 teaspoon fennel seeds,
 coarsely ground
$^1/_2$ teaspoon turmeric
 powder
$^1/_2$ teaspoon ground
 cumin
1 teaspoon chilli powder
2 eggs, beaten
175 ml ($^2/_3$ cup) water
1 large onion, finely
 chopped
2 teaspoons grated ginger
3 green finger-length
 chillies, finely chopped
2 sprigs curry leaves,
 finely chopped
1 spring onion, finely
 sliced
500 g (1 lb) small
 prawns, shelled and
 deveined
Oil for deep-frying

1 Sift the flours, baking powder, salt, fennel, turmeric, cumin and chilli powders into a large mixing bowl. Make a well in the centre, add the eggs and water and stir to make a smooth, thick batter.
2 Stir in the chopped onion, ginger, chillies, curry leaves, spring onion and prawns and set aside for 20 minutes to marinate.
3 Heat the oil in a frying pan over medium-high heat until quite hot. Drop 1 tablespoon at a time of the prawn batter into the hot oil and fry on both sides until golden brown, about 2 minutes.
4 Remove and drain on absorbent paper. Serve hot with chutney or sweet chilli sauce.

Semolina is the ground core of the durum wheat grains and has a bland flavour and slightly coarse texture. Semolina, both coarse and fine, is used in many Indian sweets and some bread and is also used in making pasta. It is available in the baking sections of most supermarkets.

Channa flour is made by milling hulled Indian channa dal. It is very fine in texture and pale yellow in colour. It can be obtained from Indian grocers and health-food stores. Finely ground chickpea flour may be used as a substitute.

Serves 6
Preparation time: **40 mins**   Cooking time: **20 mins**

Make a well in the centre of the flour mixture and add the eggs and water.

Drop 1 tablespoon at a time of the batter into the hot oil and fry on both sides.

Coriander Chicken

1 chicken, skinned and cut into serving pieces
1 teaspoon chilli powder
1 teaspoon salt
250 ml (1 cup) plain yoghurt
2 tablespoons oil
3 large onions, finely chopped
2 tablespoons fresh ginger paste
2 tablespoons garlic paste
5 green finger-length chillies (more if desired), finely chopped
2 tablespoons coriander powder
1 teaspoon cumin powder
200 g (4 cups) finely chopped fresh coriander leaves
100 g ($2^1/_2$ cups) fresh mint leaves, washed and chopped fine

1 Mix the chicken pieces with the chilli powder, salt and half of the yoghurt. Marinate for 15 minutes. (Reserve the remainder of the yogurt for later use.)
2 In a large saucepan or wok, heat the oil over medium heat and stir-fry the onions until transparent before adding the ginger and garlic paste. Stir-fry until fragrant, about 5 minutes. Add the green chillies, coriander and cumin powders, stirring well into the onion mixture.
3 Drain the chicken pieces and add to the pan. Increase the heat to high and stir-fry for 5 minutes. Stir constantly to prevent sticking and burning.
4 Scrape the leftover marinade from the bowl into the cooking chicken pieces, and add the remaining yoghurt. Add the chopped coriander and mint leaves and mix well.
5 Bring to a boil, then cover with a lid, reduce the heat to low and cook until the chicken pieces are done, about 20 to 25 minutes. Serve hot.

Serves 4–6
Preparation time: 20 mins
Cooking time: 25 mins

Fiery Chicken Vindaloo

2 tablespoons ghee or butter
1 medium onion
50 g (1 cup) finely chopped fresh coriander leaves
1 chicken, skinned and cut into serving pieces
1 teaspoon salt
2 large or 3 medium potatoes, boiled until cooked, then
  peeled and quartered

Masala Paste
1 tablespoon cumin seeds
8 to 12 dried red chillies, soaked until soft and cut into
  lengths
1 cm ($1/2$ in) fresh turmeric root, peeled
5 cardamom pods
10 cloves garlic
3 tablespoons white vinegar

1 To make the Masala Paste, grind the ingredients in
a blender until smooth.
2 Heat the ghee in a large wok over medium heat and
fry the onion until lightly browned. Add the chopped
coriander leaves and stir-fry until aromatic, about
3 minutes.
3 Stir in the blended Masala Paste and stir-fry over
low heat until the oil separates.
4 Add the chicken pieces and salt, stirring well to
coat the chicken pieces with the Masala Paste. Cover,
reduce the heat to low, and simmer until the chicken
is done, for about 20 to 25 minutes, stirring occasionally.
5 Add the boiled potatoes, mix well and serve with
Coriander Coconut Chutney (see page 5).

Serves 4–6
Preparation time: **15 mins**
Cooking time: **30 mins**

Andhra Chicken Curry

12 shallots, peeled
5 cm (2 in) fresh ginger
10 cloves garlic
1 teaspoon cumin seeds
1 teaspoon black
  peppercorns
2 dried red chillies, cut
  into lengths
150 g (1 1/2 cups) grated
  fresh coconut
1 chicken, skinned and
  washed, cut into serving
  pieces
5 tablespoons oil
1 cinnamon stick
5 cloves
8 cardamom pods
1 teaspoon cumin
1 onion, finely sliced
150 g (1 cup) diced fresh
  or canned tomatoes
1 teaspoon turmeric
  powder
250 ml (1 cup) water
1/2 teaspoon salt
50 g (1 cup) coriander
  leaves, chopped

1 Grind the shallots, ginger, garlic, cumin, black peppercorns, dried chillies and grated coconut in a blender until fine, adding a bit of the oil if necessary to keep the mixture turning. Add the spice mix to the chicken pieces in a bowl and coat well. Set aside to marinate for 20 minutes.

2 In a large pot, heat the oil and stir-fry the cinnamon, cloves, cardamons and cumin until aromatic. Add the onion and stir-fry over low heat until golden brown, about 3 minutes. Stir in the tomatoes and continue to cook until the oil separates, about 5 minutes.

3 Add the chicken pieces with the marinade and the turmeric powder, stirring well to blend the chicken with the cooked spices, about 2 minutes.

4 Add the water and salt and cook until the chicken is tender, about 20 minutes.

5 Garnish with the coriander leaves and serve.

Serves 4–6
Preparation: 35 mins
Cooking time: 40 mins

Shredded Chicken Fry

3 green finger-length chillies, chopped
4 cloves garlic
2 cm (³/₄ in) fresh ginger
2 onions, diced
1 tablespoon vinegar or lime juice
2 chicken breasts, skinned and shredded
2 tablespoons oil
1 teaspoon cumin seeds
1 teaspoon fennel seeds
3 tablespoons cumin powder
1 teaspoon salt
1 tablespoon freshly ground black pepper

1 Grind the green chillies, garlic, ginger, onions and vinegar to a paste in a blender. In a large bowl, stir the paste into the shredded chicken and leave to marinate in the refrigerator for an hour or so.

2 Heat the oil in a pan and stir-fry the cumin and fennel seeds until aromatic. Add in the marinated chicken pieces along with the marinade. Stir in the cumin powder, salt and pepper and mix well, continuing to cook until the chicken is done and fairly dry.

Serves 4
Preparation time: 15 mins
Cooking time: 20 mins

Chilli Pork Fry

2 tablespoons oil
1 teaspoon fennel seeds,
  slightly crushed
1 teaspoon cumin seeds
2 medium onions, diced
4 dried red chillies,
  cut into pieces
2 ripe tomatoes, thinly
  sliced
2 cloves garlic, minced
3 green finger-length
  chillies, sliced
2 teaspoons chilli powder
500 g (1 lb) pork, cubed
1 tablespoon vinegar
1 teaspoon salt

1 Heat the oil in a wok or skillet and stir-fry the fennel and cumin seeds until aromatic, then add the onions and stir-fry until golden brown, about 10 minutes in total.

2 Add the chillies, sliced tomato, ginger and garlic and stir-fry over low heat until the oil separates. Add the rest of the ingredients except the vinegar and cook until the pork is tender, about 20 minutes.

3 Just before removing from the heat, add the vinegar, mix well and serve.

Serves 4
Preparation time: **15 mins**
Cooking time: **40 mins**

Mutton or Lamb Masala

4 tablespoons oil
2 short cinnamon sticks
6 cardamom pods
6 cloves
1 teaspoon fennel seeds
1 onion, peeled and
  sliced
2 ripe tomatoes, diced
1 tablespoon meat curry
  powder
2 teaspoons garam
  masala (see note)
1 tablespoon coriander
  powder
500 ml (2 cups) water
500 g (1 lb) mutton or
  lamb, cubed
1 teaspoon salt

Spice Paste
2 onions, sliced
3 cm (1 in) ginger
2 cloves garlic
1 teaspoon black
  peppercorns
2 sprigs curry leaves,
  removed from stalk
5 dried red chillies, cut
  into lengths
20 g ($^1/_2$ cup) mint
  leaves
25 g ($^1/_2$ cup) fresh
  coriander leaves

1 Grind the Spice Paste ingredients in a blender until fine. Set aside.
2 Heat the oil in a wok over medium heat and fry the cinnamon, cardamoms, cloves and fennel until aromatic. Add the onion and tomatoes and stir-fry until the onion turns golden brown, about 3 minutes.
3 Stir in the ground Spice Paste, the meat curry powder, garam masala and coriander powder. Add the water and mutton or lamb. Cook until the meat is tender and the liquid evaporates, about 30 minutes. Season with salt to taste.

Garam masala is an Indian blend of powdered spices, usually including cinnamon, cardamon, cloves, fennel and black pepper. Pre-blended *garam masala* can be bought from any store specializing in spices. Store in an airtight jar away from heat or sunlight.

Serves 4
Preparation time: **40 mins**
Cooking time: **35 mins**

Country-style Lamb Curry

2 teaspoons + 3 tablespoons oil
2 onions, chopped
1 large ripe tomato, diced
3 tablespoons coriander seeds
2 dried red chillies, soaked in water, drained
200 ml (³/₄ cup) water
1 teaspoon mustard seeds
1 teaspoon fennel seeds
2 onions, peeled and sliced
1 sprig curry leaves
2 ripe tomatoes, quartered
500 g (1 lb) boneless lamb or beef, cubed
500 ml (2 cups) thick coconut milk
250 ml (1 cup) water
25 g (¹/₂ cup) coriander leaves, chopped
1 teaspoon salt

1 Heat 2 teaspoons of the oil in a skillet and fry the onions, diced tomato, coriander seeds and dried chillies until aromatic, about 3 minutes. Cool thoroughly and grind to a paste in a blender with the 200 ml (³/₄ cup) water and set aside.
2 Heat the remaining oil and fry the mustard and fennel seeds until aromatic. Add the onion slices and curry leaves and stir-fry until the onion turns brown. Add the ground spice paste, the tomato quarters and the cubed meat. Stir-fry until the meat changes colour.
3 Add the coconut milk, the remaining 250 ml (1 cup) water and the coriander leaves and cook, stirring frequently, until the meat is tender, about 30 minutes for lamb and 45 minutes for beef (add more water if using beef and the curry becomes too dry). Season with the salt, and serve.

Serves 4
Preparation time: **15 mins**
Cooking time: **40 mins (lamb) or 50 mins (beef)**

Mutton Soup

2 tablespoons oil
2 short cinnamon sticks
6 cardamom pods
6 cloves
1 teaspoon fennel seeds
1 onion, thinly sliced
2 sprigs curry leaves
500 g (1 lb) mutton ribs or 300 g (10 oz) lamb meat
2 teaspoons ginger paste
2 teaspoons garlic paste
2 green finger-length chillies, chopped
1 teaspoon turmeric powder
2 tablespoons meat curry powder
$1^1/_2$ litres (6 cups) water
1 potato, peeled and cubed
1 carrot, cubed
40 g ($^3/_4$ cup) chopped coriander leaves
40 g (1 cup) chopped mint leaves
1 teaspoon salt, or to taste

1 In a large pan, heat the oil and fry the cinnamon, cardamoms, cloves and fennel until aromatic, about 3 minutes. Add the onion and curry leaves and stir-fry for a further 5 minutes until the onion is golden brown.
2 Add the meat, ginger and garlic pastes, the green chillies, spice powders and water. Bring to a boil, then simmer over low heat until the meat is tender, about $1^1/_2$ hours.
4 Add the vegetables, herbs and salt 30 minutes before the end of cooking. Adjust the salt to taste and serve.

Serves 4–6
Preparation time: **20 mins**
Cooking time: **$1^1/_2$ hours**

Meatballs in Spicy Curry Gravy

500 g (1 lb) minced lamb or beef
1 onion, finely chopped
1 tablespoon ginger paste
4 green finger-length chillies, minced
2 tablespoons channa flour
1 teaspoon salt
3 tablespoons oil
1 teaspoon mustard seeds
1 onion, peeled and sliced
2 sprigs curry leaves
625 ml (2^1/$_2$ cups) thin coconut milk
125 ml (^{1}/$_2$ cup) thick coconut milk
^{1}/$_2$ teaspoon salt
3 tablespoons lime juice

Spice Paste

3 tablespoons coriander seeds
2 teaspoons sesame seeds
5 dried red chillies, cut into lengths
4 cloves garlic
1 tablespoon ginger
1^1/$_2$ teaspoons garam masala
1 teaspoon black pepper powder
1^1/$_2$ teaspoons cumin powder

1 To make the meatballs, combine the minced lamb or beef with the onions, ginger, chillies, channa flour and salt. Mix well and shape into round balls. Set aside.

2 To prepare the Spice Paste, first dry-fry the coriander seeds, sesame seeds and dried chillies in a wok or skillet over low heat for 3 to 4 minutes until lightly browned and fragrant. Allow to cool and then grind them with the garlic and ginger in a blender until fine. Stir in the garam masala, black pepper and cumin powders and mix well. Set aside.

3 Heat the oil in a pan and fry the mustard seeds until they pop. Add the onion slices and curry leaves, then stir-fry until the onion browns, about 3 minutes. Add the spice paste and stir-fry until the oil separates, about 5 minutes.

4 Add the thin coconut milk and gently put in the prepared meatballs. Simmer over gentle heat until the meatballs are cooked, about 20 minutes.

5 Add the thick coconut milk and bring to a boil and simmer for 1 minute. Season with salt to taste. Turn off the heat and stir in the lime juice. Serve hot with rice or bread.

Serves 4
Preparation time: 40 mins
Cooking time: 30 mins

Recipe List

Chutney

Coriander Coconut
Chutney 5

Spicy Mango Coconut
Chutney 5

Sweet Lime Chutney 4

Sweet Tomato Date
Chutney 4

Seafood

Curried Crabs 33

Fish Sothi Curry 44

Kerala Fish Curry 35

Masala Grilled
Fish 41

Prawn Curry 31

Prawn Fritters 46

Salt Fish Mango Curry 43

Swordfish Curry 36

Tamarind Crab Soup 39

Tanjore Fried Fish 40

Meat

Chilli Pork Fry 55

Country-style
Lamb Curry 58

Meatballs in Spicy Curry
Gravy 63

Mutton or Lamb
Masala 57

Mutton Soup 60

Poultry

Andhra Chicken Curry 52

Coriander Chicken 49

Fiery Chicken
Vindaloo 50

Shredded Chicken
Fry 54

Rice and Bread

Chapati 10

Flat Bread 10

Fragrant Mint Rice 6

Plain Basmati Rice 6

Potato Puri 8

Vegetables

Banana Stem
Curry 24

Fragrant Eggplant
Curry 18

Garlic Curry 13

Potato and Baby Whitebait
Masala 27

Sambar 16

Spicy Rasam Carrot
Soup 21

Spicy Tomato Soup 14

Spinach with Dal and
Dried Prawn Curry 29

Stir-fried Ladies
Fingers 13

Vegetarian Dal Curry 23

Vegetable Stew 16

Vegetables in Spicy
Coconut Milk 26